My Day in the
FOREST

Jory Randall

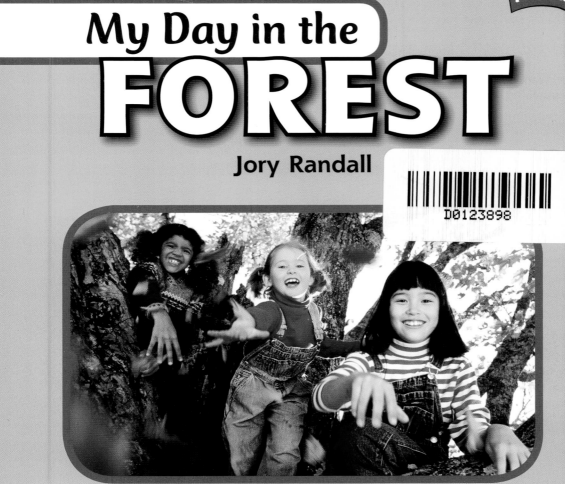

PowerKiDS press™

New York

Published in 2010 by The Rosen Publishing Group, Inc.
29 East 21st Street, New York, NY 10010

First Edition

Editor: Joanne Randolph
Book Design: Julio Gil
Photo Researcher: Jessica Gerweck

Photo Credits: Cover, p. 7 © Tom Stewart/Corbis; p. 5 © Benelux/zefa/Corbis; p. 9 Amy Eckert/ Getty Images; p. 11 Anne Ackermann/Getty Images; p. 13 © John-Francis Bourke/zefa/Corbis; p. 15 Patrick Molnar/Getty Images; p. 17 Charles Gupton/Getty Images; p. 19 LWA/Getty Images; p. 21 Altrendo Images/Getty Images; p. 23 © www.iStockphoto.com/lightasafeather; p. 24 (top left) © www.iStockphoto.com/ballycroy; p. 24 (top right, bottom right) © www.iStockphoto.com/AVTG; p. 24 (bottom left) © www.iStockphoto.com/rhyman007.

Library of Congress Cataloging-in-Publication Data

Randall, Jory.
  My day in the forest / Jory Randall.
      p. cm. — (A kid's life!)
  Includes index.
  ISBN 978-1-4042-8078-6 (library binding) — ISBN 978-1-4358-2475-1 (pbk.) — ISBN 978-1-4358-2476-8 (6-pack)
  1. Forests and forestry—Recreational use—Juvenile literature. I. Title.
  GV191.67.F6R36 2010
  719'.33—dc22
                                        2008052900

Manufactured in the United States of America

Contents

Have you ever been to the **forest**? I love going to the forest with my family for the day.

We go hiking in the forest. Hiking means we walk on the **trails** and paths in the woods.

Some paths are big and wide.
They are easy to hike.

Some forest trails are rocky or bumpy. It is harder to hike these trails, but it is still fun!

We like to climb trees when we are in the forest. How high can you climb?

We search for bugs in the forest. They are fun to watch before we set them free.

I like to fish when I am in the forest. Sometimes I catch a fish but not every time.

The forest that I go to has a **river** in it. My family likes to ride in a **canoe** down the river.

We ride our bikes when we go to the forest. Sometimes we stop to rest and take a look around.

The forest is a fun place to learn and discover new things. What will you see in the forest?

Words to Know

canoe

forest

river

trail

Index

Web Sites

Due to the changing nature of Internet links, PowerKids Press has developed an online list of Web sites related to the subject of this book. This site is updated regularly. Please use this link to access the list:
www.powerkidslinks.com/kidlife/forest/